A gift for:

From:

Helen Exley

Other books in this series:
365 Days with my bossy Cat   Friendship 365
365 The Secrets of Happiness   For my Mother 365
Other giftbooks by Helen Exley:
❤ Dogs   Utterly Wonderful Dogs   Woof!
❤ Cats   Utterly Adorable Cats   Meow!

Published in 2012 and 2022 by Helen Exley® LONDON in Great Britain.

Edited by Dalton Exley

Photography copyright © Yoneo Morita 2012 and Hanadeka™
Licensed through Intercontinental Licensing
Words by Pam Brown © Helen Exley Creative Ltd 2012, 2022.
Design, selection and arrangement © Helen Exley Creative Ltd 2012, 2022.

ISBN 978-1-78485-333-4

12 11 10 9 8 7 6 5 4 3 2 1

Helen Exley® LONDON, 16 Chalk Hill, Watford, Herts WD19 4BG, UK
www.helenexley.com

MIX
Paper from
responsible sources
FSC® C081635

The dog was created especially for children.

HENRY WARD BEECHER (1813-1887)

If you love this book...

... you will probably want to know how to find other

HELEN EXLEY® LONDON

books like it. They're all listed on

www.helenexley.com

Helen Exley and her team have specialised in creating gifts
between families, friends and loved ones...
A major part of Helen's work has been to bring love and communication
within families by finding and publishing the things people everywhere
would like to say to the people they love.
Her books obviously strike a chord because they are now
distributed in more than eighty countries.

JANUARY 2

A dog's love
is unconditional
and its
companionship
unsurpassed.

ANNABEL GOLDSMITH

DECEMBER 31

To buy a pup
is to invest in love.

PAM BROWN, B.1928

JANUARY 3

Dogs want and need what we do: friends, sunshine, play and love.

JEFFREY MASSON, B. 1941

DECEMBER 30

He toils not, neither does he spin, yet Solomon in all his glory never lay upon a door-mat all day long, sun-soaked and fly-fed and fat, while his master worked... to purchase an idle wag of the Solomonic tail, seasoned with a look of tolerant recognition.

AMBROSE BIERCE (1842-C.1914)

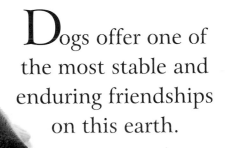

Dogs offer one of
the most stable and
enduring friendships
on this earth.

WILLARD SCOTT

DECEMBER 29

Choosing a puppy is a most difficult task – it's impossible not to fall in love with every one you see.

STUART & LINDA MACFARLANE

JANUARY 5

There is always
one dog in your life
that is the gatekeeper;
the one who opens
your heart
to others.

PETER EGAN

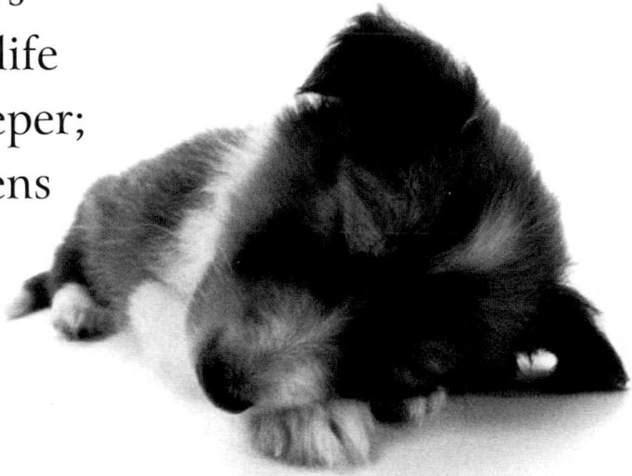

DECEMBER 28

[My dogs have] filled such a lonely hole in my life, my constant companions, I can't imagine how I would cope if I were to lose them. They're funny, affectionate and full of the kind of energy that tends to diminish with age and illness. They're a daily injection of joie de vivre.

JENNI MURRAY

JANUARY 6

The smallest of dogs
can fill a room with love
and healing and their
very presence in the home
can eliminate
depression or sadness.

BILLY ROBERTS, FROM
"THE HEALING PAW"

Your dog will
love you no matter
what you have become.

BEL MOONEY

He was a very
bad boy yet
with a heart
as boundless as
a summer sky.

JOHN GROGAN

Although [human and dogs] have much in common, they also complement each other by doing, viewing, and experiencing life in vastly different ways. They make up for each other's abilities or inabilities to cope with and thrive on this planet. No wonder dogs and humans had to find each other.

ALLEN & LINDA ANDERSON

A dog has
one aim in life.
To bestow
his heart.

J. R. ACKERLEY (1896-1967)

DECEMBER 25

There is nothing like the loyalty and love dogs have for their families. Nothing.

MARK R. LEVIN

No matter where
you are, your dog
will welcome you home.

BEL MOONEY

DECEMBER 24

Adog is a chance to
express yourself without
the fear of seeming foolish,
a chance to share emotions
that others of our kind
too often repel
– tenderness,
outright joy, love.

GAIL PETERSEN

A dog wags its tail
with its heart.

MARTIN BUXBAUM

DECEMBER 23

One rattle of the biscuit tin and you've got friends for life. They sit and stare with solemn eyes, and if you don't take the hint, you get barked at.

JANINE CHUBB, AGE 10

One can only slip down so deep in one's thoughts when a dog is around.

ROY MACGREGOR

DECEMBER 22

Tests have in fact shown that simply stroking your dog... helps to normalize blood pressure, and can also help to lower stress levels.

BILLY ROBERTS,
FROM "THE HEALING PAW"

JANUARY 12

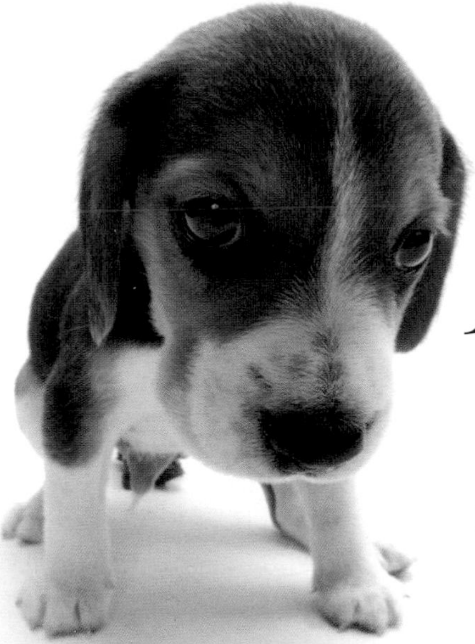

Anyone who adopts a pet can learn something about faith, hope, and love.

CHRISTOPHER S. WREN

DECEMBER 21

He is going to stick to you, to comfort you, guard you, and give his life for you, if need be.... You are his pal.

JEROME K. JEROME (1859-1927)

There is simply
no down to dog.

ROY MACGREGOR

DECEMBER 20

Life without our dogs
would be very empty.
They are affectionate,
entertaining and give you
the most wonderful greeting
when you come home.

WILLIAM ROACHE

JANUARY 14

They ask so little
in return for what
they give, yet they
give so much,
and they give in silence.

JOHN O'HURLEY

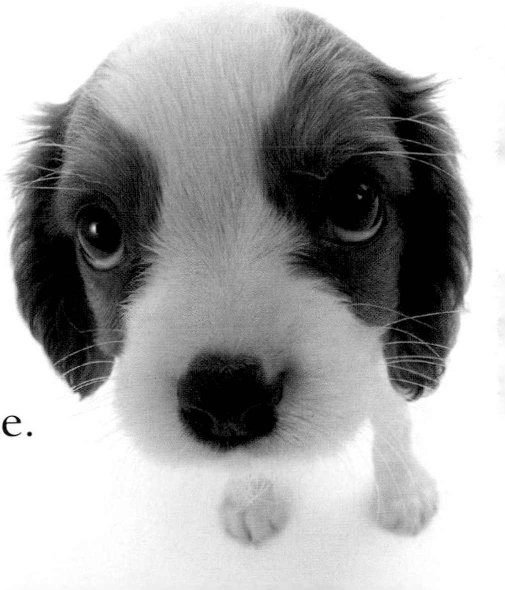

DECEMBER 19

Whihile I run my toes over his arched spine, I actually feel my tension easing and my bunched up muscles relaxing. I imagine (as most dog owners invariably do) that he "understands" me, understands what I'm saying to him.

SHOBHA DÉ,
FROM "SPEEDPOST"

Dogs don't
do grumpy.

JENNI MURRAY

Dogs effortlessly exhibit an ease of well-being that philosophers and seekers have thirsted after for eternity.

MARI GAYATRI STEIN

Dogs want and need
to be loved.

STEPHEN WINN

Dogs are our link to paradise. They don't know evil or jealously or discontent. To sit with a dog on a hillside on a glorious afternoon is to be back in Eden, where doing nothing was not boring – it was peace.

MILAN KUNDERA, B. 1929

A dog's only
ambition is
to give you
all his love.

STUART & LINDA MACFARLANE

DECEMBER 16

My dogs have taught me so much – patience, unconditional love, and, of course, compassion. Additionally, they always remind me of the secret to happiness. They are fully present. They rejoice at everything – being with the ones they love, the same landscape they've seen a hundred times, or catching some scent in the air. I am constantly learning from them to slow down, be appreciative, and enjoy things exactly as they are.

RORY FREEDMAN

They exude gratitude with every windshield-wiper wag of their tails, and clear away the mists of our discontent.

MARI GAYATRI STEIN

DECEMBER 15

One of the underrated pleasures of having a dog, as I'd come to appreciate, was the cover it gives you for talking freely and fluidly to yourself. Having another body around, especially one who reacts to the sound of your voice – and won't take you on about the content – was far more appealing and comforting that I'd expected.

STEPHEN WINN

Walking your dog
is life affirming…
It's as if you're plaited
together, one extended
consciousness, awareness
overlapping.

BRUCE FOGLE

DECEMBER 14

What dogs do – particularly a middle-aged, confident, contented dog – is offer perspective. They can cause you to look at something from another angle, to realize, in an instant, how lucky you are.

ROY MACGREGOR

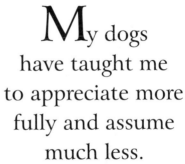

My dogs
have taught me
to appreciate more
fully and assume
much less.

JOHN O'HURLEY

DECEMBER 13

There is something
consoling about stroking
a pet when you feel
frightened and alone.

CHRISTOPHER S. WREN

JANUARY 21

All knowledge,
the totality of all questions
and answers,
is contained in the dog.

FRANZ KAFKA (1883-1924)

Once a dog loves you,
it loves you always,
no matter what you do, no
matter what happens,
no matter how much time
goes by.

JEFFREY MASSON, B. 1941

JANUARY 22

There's something very touching about an animal that is dependent on you for everything.

PHILIP TREACY

DECEMBER 11

He became the focal point of our existence. If he knew a walk was imminent, he would leap in pure bliss like a ballet dancer.

LEO MCKINSTRY, FROM "DAILY MAIL", FEBRUARY 18, 2003

She was joyous and beautiful and a constant symbol of happiness. Although she obviously emulated us, sometimes I wonder. Shouldn't I have emulated her?

BROOKS ATKINSON (1894-1984)

"Go away, you bad, bad dog." And so he would, crawling across the carpet on his belly, ears down, abject.

PAM BROWN, B. 1928

Dogs can tell
when they're
around dog lovers.

MARK R. LEVIN

DECEMBER 9

Dogs are
fantastic stress
relievers.

ALLEN & LINDA ANDERSON

Without dogs the world would seem a lonely place....

LOYD GROSSMAN,
FROM "THE DOG'S TALE"

DECEMBER 8

If I was upset or blue, he'd dote on me, put his head in my lap and... throw a paw over my leg, or follow me around the house. When I'd bawled the night before, he'd stuck to me like glue. He'd even tried to distract me by bringing over a ball, then grabbing his leash and dropping it at my feet.

STEVE DUNO

They recognize that we provide for them what they cannot provide for themselves. They love us for the kindness of that responsibility. We love them for the joy and affection that they return. It is a perfect, constantly renewing circle.

JOHN O'HURLEY

One looks at
a sleeping puppy
– and forgives
it everything.

PAM BROWN, B.1928

Dogs don't
bear grudges.

SUE TOWNSEND

DECEMBER 6

Our friendship
defined us. These days
I can't think of myself,
or of life before or after him,
without imagining him here
forever, like an inscription
carved into my heart.

STEVE DUNO

JANUARY 28

A dog: companion, friend, protector, playmate and life-changer. Dogs add a dimension to our lives that otherwise would be just a vacant spot. They work for us, guard us, play with us, entertain us, love us, keep us company, and change our lives.

H. NORMAN WRIGHT

Nirvana must be very like a replete puppy's sleep. A rapture beyond dreams.

PAM BROWN, B.1928

JANUARY 29

Go into the park
on your own and start
talking to strangers,
and people will think
you are at best a sad,
lonely git, and at worst
a child molester. Go in
with a dog and
everybody talks to you.

ELINOR GOODMAN

Happiness is a warm puppy.

CHARLES M. SCHULZ
(1922-2000)

Dogs are healers. They are enlightened. They seem to have figured out how to live beautifully so much better than we humans have. While we struggle to figure out why we were put here on Earth, all a dog wants is to love and be loved – a powerful lesson for us all.

DR. BERNIE S. SIEGEL

However much humans may do for a dog, there is always a bit of them which remains doggedly independent of any owner – shared or otherwise.

ELINOR GOODMAN

A pup does
not know words.
It just hears love.

PAMELA DUGDALE

DECEMBER 2

A dog has an uncanny ability of turning a lonely moment into one where there's a companion who never takes life too seriously for too long.

JENNI MURRAY

I realized I hadn't experienced much love, joy, and exuberance in years. She brought with her zest for life and a playfulness that ignited a spark in me that I'd let fizzle without realizing it.

SAGE LEWIS

I seem to spend a great deal of time just staring at the dog, struck by how mysterious and beautiful she is to me and by how much my world has changed since she came along.

CAROLINE KNAPP

O ur dogs...gave us
the gifts of love, protection
and comfort in the sad and
tough time....Dogs really
are our very best friends.

WILLARD SCOTT

Dog love
is powerful stuff.

JON KATZ

FEBRUARY 3

In dogs, we find true and faithful companions, who love you whether you are a vagrant living under a bridge or the richest person in the world.

RYAN O'MEARA

...give up their affections and
their devotion recklessly
and serve to show us in a tangible
way something that transcends
what we know of other imperfect
loves in this workaday world
of demands and disappointments.
Their message is simple.
They are here to remind us,
"You are loved."

SHANE GALLOWAY

I've always believed that life is rubbish without a dog to come home to. No matter what kind of day you've had, they're always delighted to see you.

CAROLINE QUENTIN

NOVEMBER 28

The dog chooses us, not because it is confused about our identity, not because dogs think we are the marvel of creation, but merely because dogs love us. Dogs love us not only because we feed them, or walk them, or groom them, or protect them, but because we are fun.

JEFFREY MASSON, B. 1941

As diverse as
each of us are,
a love for dogs brings
people together.

WILLARD SCOTT

I hugged him to me, nestling into his soft, downy coat, then placing a kiss on top of his head. He snuggled in, and as I felt the love coming from this wee pup, I realised that here was someone who would let me love him back.

NILALA GARDENER

It doesn't take much to make a dog happy: just the little things, the basic things. It is an important life lesson dogs teach us, and my dogs taught me.

MARK R. LEVIN

It is by muteness that a dog becomes for one so utterly beyond value... where words play no torturing tricks... Those are the moments that I think are precious to a dog – when, with his adoring soul coming through his eyes, he feels that you are really thinking of him.

JOHN GALSWORTHY (1867-1933)

FEBRUARY 7

This enigmatic animal that stumbled into my life... gave me reason to pause, to slow down, to relax, and to pay mind to the fullness of my life.

SHANE GALLOWAY

At moments of grief, Arthur would put his head on my knee, or lie like a huge beanbag on my feet. He was also my unofficial personal trainer, forcing me to walk three times a day, every day, whatever the weather.

ESTHER RANTZEN, B. 1940

Dogs belong to that elite group of con artists at the very pinnacle of their profession, the ones who pick our pockets clean and leave us smiling about it.

STEPHEN BUDIANSKY

How small,
how helpless,
how utterly
gormless
a puppy is.

CHARLOTTE GRAY

Dogs, like children, become emblems for who we are out in the world. We can't help letting it happen.

STEVEN WINN

Money will buy
a pretty good dog but
it won't buy the wag
of his tail.

JOSH BILLINGS (1818-1885)

B uy a pup
and your money
will buy love
unflinching.

RUDYARD KIPLING
(1865-1936)

NOVEMBER 22

It is strange how so miniature a creature can fill so large a space with his presence. His absolute trust calls forth absolute benevolence; and though, strictly speaking, he is a parasite, in truth we are as dependent upon him as he is on us.

THEODORE DALRYMPLE

Dogs... bring us
back to life, haul us
into the present, make
us get on with things
instead of moping.

BEL MOONEY

Your dog is your only philosopher.

PLATO (C.427-348 B.C.)

Dogs allow you to express your emotions in a very straightforward way.

JUDITH SUMMERS

What do they want in return for the happiness they bring us? Love, unconditional love. A head to be scratched, a tummy to be rubbed, a ball to be thrown or a place on the couch. Not too much to be asked from a loyal friend. A loyal family member.

LONG ISLAND PETER

FEBRUARY 13

He never sulks, never mopes, never shows me anything other than the deepest affection.

RICK STEIN

He looked at me with the most soulful eyes and I felt his comfort when he was in my arms.

ANNA LUPACCHINO

What joy they have brought.
What companions. In a frantic and
demanding life, my dogs have been
a sanctuary. Far from any
judgement and expectation,
they offer unconditional
love – and I seem
to mean as much to
them as they mean to me.

JACKIE STEWART, B. 1939

A puppy can often bring out the puppy in an aged dog.

JEFFREY MASSON, B. 1941

FEBRUARY 15

What is it that cats, humans and dogs have in common? Our devotion to love.

JEFFREY MASSON, B. 1941

Dogs are the best.
And as you say,
their entire existence
is to give us love
and pleasure.
They are selfless.

MARK R. LEVIN

FEBRUARY 16

Dogs seem to see into our souls and offer us kindness, devotion, and complete acceptance. We talk to them and sing to them and take them on rides in the car because we know they like the car.

MARY TIEGREEN

Dogs have no guile...
They don't profess to love
your work and then attack it.
They don't lick you then bite
to draw blood. In a world
of hypocrisy and betrayal,
dogs are direct. They never lie.

ERICA JONG, B. 1942

I truly believe God created dogs for a cause. They are the greatest companions a man could ever have.

MICKEY ROURKE

Dogs are ready, to forgive
anything we do to them.

JEFFREY MASSON, B. 1941

Don't make the mistake of treating your dogs like humans, or they'll treat you like dogs.

MARTHA SCOTT

NOVEMBER 14

I would often get down on the floor, hold either Pepsi or Sprite's head in my hands, and put my nose up against their nose. I would tell them how beautiful they are, how much I love them, and kiss them on the nose. They would stare into my eyes and seem to know exactly what I was saying and feeling. And I know they loved me, too.

MARK R. LEVIN

FEBRUARY 19

It doesn't surprise me
to discover that people who
have a close and affectionate
relationship with a dog suffer
less stress, are less likely
to suffer a heart attack and,
if they do, are more likely
to recover.

JENNI MURRAY

NOVEMBER 13

He had spent his life giving everyone around him love, affection, and happiness.

MARK R. LEVIN

The dog is the only being
that loves you more
than you love yourself.

FRITZ VON UNRUH

NOVEMBER 12

No matter how we treat them, what we do to them, how little attention we pay to them; they are anxious to please us, eager to be with us.

JEFFREY MASSON, B. 1941

FEBRUARY 21

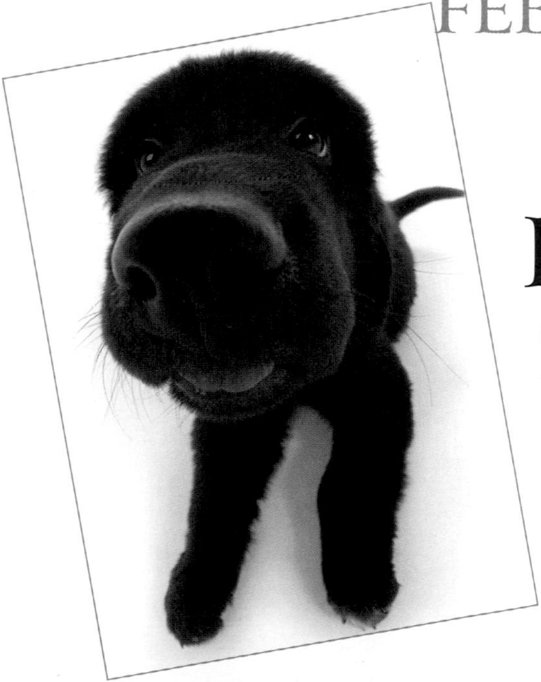

Frankie and my other dogs have taught me that life is abundant in beauty and love.

BARBARA TECHEL

NOVEMBER 11

No other animal mourns for a lost human friend in the way that a dog does. You cannot impress your dog with beauty, wealth, possessions, power, or physical prowess. We might fall in love with somebody for any of these qualities. A dog does not fall in love, the dog merely loves.

JEFFREY MASSON, B. 1941

FEBRUARY 22

Dogs and cats are my passion. Their love is unchanging, unconditional, and unbounding in warm kisses and wiggling bodies.

GINGER ROGERS (1911-1995)

This dog would never be a mere pet. She would be more like a force, a way of life, a way of looking at things, a friend, an inspiration, an adventure. She brought us the most intense pleasure, along with the most intense agony.

PETER MARTIN

He is so shaggy.
People are amazed
when he gets up and
they suddenly realise
they have been talking
to the wrong end.

ELIZABETH JONES

He's my playmate at the park, my camping buddy, my cuddle partner.

ANNA LUPACCHINO

They have taught me to believe in the constant goodness that seems to emanate so easily from their gentle and loving nature.

JOHN O'HURLEY

Cats can tolerate us,
whereas dogs adore us.

JEFFREY MASSON, B. 1941

You can't fool a dog.
Dogs know
when you're sad.
They sense
when you need them.

ALLEN & LINDA ANDERSON

He's almost always wearing a big smile, and his long, furry tail is constantly wagging. Well, actually, when he's really happy, his tail moves in a circle much like a propeller.

MARK R. LEVIN

FEBRUARY 26

When you need to feel loved there is nothing quite like having a dog look up at you with adoring eyes.

NIGEL FARNDALE

NOVEMBER 6

Sometimes a dog
is more than a pet.
It can be a joy in good
times, a comfort in bad,
an unquestioning
friend always.

JOHN GROGAN

FEBRUARY 27

My dog, she looks
at me sometimes with that
look, and I think maybe
deep down inside
she must know exactly
how I feel. But then
maybe she just wants
the food off my plate.

AUTHOR UNKNOWN

Pets are the only creatures who give humans unconditional love. Your pet never yells at you, rejects you, tells you to go to hell or argues with you.

MARK R. LEVIN

FEBRUARY 28/29

We give dogs time
we can spare,
space we can spare,
and love we can spare.
And in return,
dogs give us their all....

M. ACKLAM

They come into our lives and bring us such joy and happiness. When we have a bad day at work, we walk through the front doors of our homes and they are there to greet us, tail wagging and butt shaking. All of a sudden that bad day doesn't mean anything.

LONG ISLAND PETER

Dogs have got us
exactly where they
want us, and we,
idiotic grins fixed
to our faces, go along
with it all.

STEPHEN BUDIANSKY

All dogs rely on their human parents to care for them – to make sure they are well fed, properly treated, and enjoy their short lives. In return, we get pure love, loyalty and happiness.

MARK R. LEVIN

The friendship and loyalty of dogs help human beings to get through just about any of life's changes and sudden curves.

ALLEN & LINDA ANDERSON

Cats can take great
pleasure in our company,
but I find it difficult to
imagine that my cats would
risk their lives to save mine.
I can easily imagine my
dogs doing this without
hesitation.

JEFFREY MASSON, B. 1941

His gentle being
calms and sustains me.
The way he runs to me
and presses into my body,
or sits quivering on my feet
at the least frightening
sound, kindles in me
the most satisfying
protective instincts.

JAN FOOK

On stubby legs he ran
to meet me, wagging his tail
like crazy, his eyes
celebrating and welcoming
my return.

JUDY MCFADDEN

MARCH 4

Pets rarely harm us at all. They love us without conditions, as a matter of course. Their love is of a pure and rare quality. For us, an indulgence. Perhaps an addiction. And when it's removed the hurt is extreme.

STEPHEN DOWNES

The dog truly loves us,
sometimes beyond
expectation, beyond measure,
beyond what we deserve,
more indeed than we love
ourselves. No dog will ever
lie to us about love.

JEFFREY MASSON, B. 1941

I loved him much more than I thought anyone could love an animal. I loved his silliness, clumsiness, kisses and protectiveness.

DIANA M. AMADEO

Dogs do not find anything "agreeable"; they are wild enthusiasts.

BEL MOONEY

When you tire of puppies...you tire of life!

AUTHOR UNKNOWN

D ogs never seem
to hold grudges against
humans.

JEFFREY MASSON, B. 1941

A relationship with
a dog also helps us know
ourselves better. A dog is
guileless and utterly
honest. It becomes
a unique mirror reflecting
us back to ourselves,
if we pay attention.

BROTHER CHRISTOPHER

I can honestly say that my life would not be complete without my beloved dogs. The most important reason is that they have taught me to recognize love.

CHRISTINE MIELE

Dogs give us
so much joy.

DEBRA BURLINGAME

OCTOBER 27

Brothers and sisters,
I bid you beware
Of giving your heart
to a dog to tear.

RUDYARD KIPLING (1865-1936)

A wise dog
can teach us much
of what we need to know.
Patience.
Caring.
Companionship.
And Love.

PAM BROWN, B.1928

From the moment I opened my front door and bent down to touch Greta's head and give her a kiss, which she exuberantly returned in Labrador fashion, I felt a special bond with her.

SALLY ROSENTHAL

Dogs are good friends;
their loyalty is unswerving.

ALLEN & LINDA ANDERSON

My goal in life
is to be as good
a person as my dog
already thinks I am.

AUTHOR UNKNOWN

Dogs come into our lives
to teach us about love
and loyalty. They depart to
teach us about loss. We try
to replace them but never
quite succeed. A new dog
never replaces an old dog;
it merely expands the heart.

ERICA JONG, B. 1942

It is hard to deny that we feel a very fundamental, innate, unlearned, and in that sense quite irrational attraction toward cute little things, especially helpless cute little things. Dogs take advantage of this no end. They play us like accordions.

STEPHEN BUDIANSKY

OCTOBER 24

He is an
affectionate, devoted
and sometimes
hilarious companion.
He has made life
worth living.

JENNI MURRAY

Maybe what I like
about dogs so much
is their appetite for life…
They are so "up",
so thrilled to see you.

MARTIN CLUNES

Goldfish, turtles and hamsters are pets. Dogs are family.

MARK R. LEVIN

Every dog owner
believes his dog
to be exceptionally
intelligent and
charming...

THEODORE DALRYMPLE

OCTOBER 22

Thoughtful dog lovers
know that to love
a dog is to know sorrow
and loss as well as joy
and companionship.
They are parts of a whole.

JON KATZ

Good dogs win
all the ribbons,
it's true.
But bad dogs
have more fun.

JOHN GROGAN

OCTOBER 21

The great thing about living with a dog is that you can lock the kitchen when you've had enough of them. But you can't really do that with a man.

LINDA MANLEY-BIRD

There's something magical about
a wet nose thrust into
your hand as you settle
down to watch TV,
and a warm healthy body
curled up at your feet.

EDWINA CURRIE, B. 1946

OCTOBER 20

The great pleasure
of a dog is that you
may make a fool
of yourself with him
and not only will
he not scold you,
but he will make
a fool of himself too.

SAMUEL BUTLER (1835-1902)

Sandy... had more than enough love for everyone.

TERESA AMBORD

Dogs love
plum cake
and affection
equally.

PAM BROWN, B. 1928

The door opens
– and her face lights up
in incredulous joy.
"You're a silly dog, then.
I told you
I wouldn't be long."
And for both of us
the world has come
right again.

PAM BROWN, B.1928

OCTOBER 18

...sun on my face, the feel of spring round the corner, and nobody anywhere in sight except a dog, are still enough to fill me with utter happiness.

ELIZABETH VON ARNIM (1866-1941)

Dogs make us
feel better.

JAN ETHERINGTON

It is always said that however
many wonderful and happy
years a dog lives,
you know that one day,
the day he dies, your dog
will break your heart.

JAMES HERRIOT (1916-1995)

Whoever said
you can't buy
happiness
forgot about
puppies.

GENE HILL

We are simply
two life forms journeying
in time in acceptance
and love for each other's
essence. And what in life
is better than that?

SANDRA LUND

Being with a dog,
understanding her moods,
her wants, her feelings,
her emotions, without
the need for words,
returns you to the core
of your being.

BRUCE FOGLE

His name is not
Wild Dog any more,
but the First Friend,
because he will be
our friend for always
and always
and always.

RUDYARD KIPLING
(1865-1936)

Dogs have an enormous capacity for helping people forget their worries and anxieties.

ALLEN & LINDA ANDERSON

OCTOBER 14

*So my good old pal,
my irregular dog,
my flea-bitten,
stub-tailed friend,
Has become a part
of my very heart,
to be cherished till
life-time's end.*

W. DAYTON WEDGEFARTH

MARCH 22

Dogs give us
so much devotion
and loyalty in return
for our care.

AUTHOR UNKNOWN

OCTOBER 13

A quiet gentle dog will bring a quiet, deep satisfaction to your whole life.

HELEN EXLEY

Every dog
would have a home,
and every home
would have a dog.

AUTHOR UNKNOWN

N̄o one with good dogs is ever truly alone.

JON KATZ

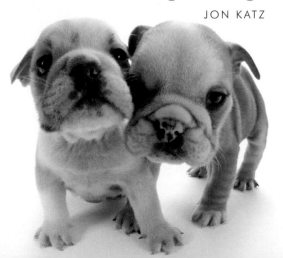

MARCH 24

A very small dog can fill a very great gap in one's life.

PAM BROWN, B.1928

A dog is all heart.
And stomach.

PAM BROWN, B.1928

Dogs...teach us to stop thinking of ourselves; they take away our self-pretence and make us live in the moment. They are wonderful creatures, all of them.

PETER EGAN

It doesn't matter whether
we are royalty or rogues;
our dogs don't care.
What we are doesn't matter.
Who we are doesn't matter.
Our dogs reward us
with their loyalty…

JOYCE STRANGER

Sometimes a dog
comes along
that really touches
your life, and you can
never forget her.

JOHN GROGAN

Dogs know that life is too precious to go into battle over something trivial. But people do it all the time.

RYAN O'MEARA

I think perhaps one of the greatest reasons I love dogs so much is that they, like me, refuse to act their age and continue their "puppydom" for their entire lives.

PETER EGAN

OCTOBER 8

A dog can add years
to an old person's life –
someone to care for,
someone to come home
to, someone to talk to.
A dear friend.

PAM BROWN, B.1928

MARCH 28

W hen you have
a dog...in your life,
you are truly blessed
for that close kind
of bond that
you won't find
anywhere else.

JAY WILLIAMS

He will kiss the hand that has
no food to offer, he will lick the wounds
and sores that come in encounter
with the roughness of the world.
He guards the sleep of his pauper master
as if he were a prince.

SENATOR GEORGE G. VEST
(1830-1904)

He behaved like he owned me, not the reverse, and I was his property in a sense.

PHILLIP TREACY

No matter how badly we behave, or how low we feel, dogs are always there to greet us, full of loyalty and kindness.

LEO MCKINSTRY,
FROM "DAILY MAIL",
FEBRUARY 18, 2003

My two little muppets
are unbridled love and joy;
I can hardly imagine they will one
day be gone. That they love me
so unconditionally
is such a gift, one
I sometimes feel
unworthy of.

RORY FREEDMAN

The games that delight dogs entail endless repetition. Stop throwing the stick and his eyes will reproach you. "Once more. Please."

PAM BROWN, B.1928

H e is the little heartbeat
at my feet.

CHARLES PATRICK DUGAN

OCTOBER 4

A dog wilts under
the words "You bad,
bad animal."

PETER GRAY, B.1928

APRIL 1

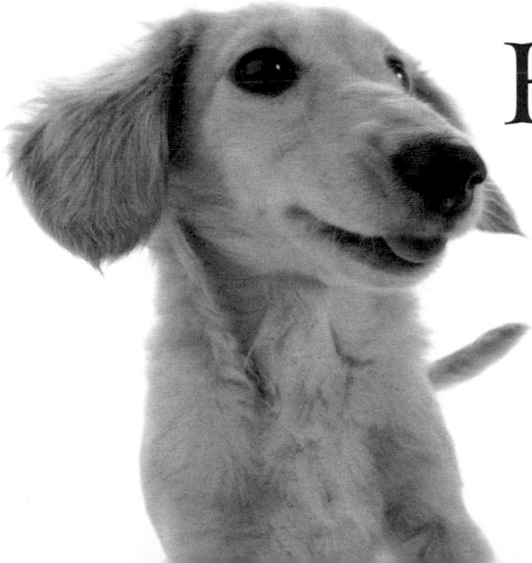

He's very affectionate
and he loves me so
much, and it's always
nice to be loved
to that degree.

JUDITH SUMMERS

The Dog will not criticize you for all your human failings. He is always there when you come home, manifestly thrilled to see you even if you have only been out to empty the dustbin for thirty seconds...

VALERIE GROVE

The beauty of having a dog, even a very old dog, is that the dog gets you out no matter what the weather, no matter what the mood.

ROY MACGREGOR

A dog will sense
when you are sad or anxious.
With a cheery,
"rufff, ruff,"
she will climb onto your lap
to lick your face....

STUART & LINDA MACFARLANE

Goofy showed me that
it is being able to give love
that we crave. A dog rejoices
in this communion:
there is no cold shoulder;
no shrinking from our touch.

BELINDA HARLEY

There is no sadder sight than a reprimanded dog. With tail between his legs and head held low he will scuffle away to a lonely solitude; waiting for your forgiveness.

STUART & LINDA MACFARLANE

Medical studies have shown that people with regular access to dogs visit the doctor less often, have lower blood pressure levels, and suffer fewer incidents of heart disease and dementia. Pet companionship can even motivate seniors to increase daily activities and socializing.

STEVE DUNO

The bond between man and dog is something that is almost absurdly strong. We who experience it feel almost ashamed to admit it to those people who do not understand or share it.

ANTHONY DANIELS

It is amazing how
much love and laughter
they bring into our lives.
Dogs are one of the wonders
of life and add
so very much to ours.
It's just the most amazing
thing to love a dog, isn't it?

JOHN GROGAN

When a dog has sprawled
in a place where someone
is bound to tread on him,
the extended paw
and pitiful whimper
can make the
inevitable appear
entirely your fault.

PAM BROWN, B.1928

Dogs are born knowing exactly what they want to do: eat, scratch, roll in disgusting stuff, sniff and squabble with other dogs, roam, sleep, have sex. Little of this is what we want them to do, of course. We ask them to sit, stay, smell pleasant, practice abstinence, and become accommodating.

JON KATZ

One of the saddest sights
is to see a Dane ill.
Their big eyes are a picture
of misery, for a sick Dane
puts on everything it can
to get all the love and sympathy.

BARBARA WOODHOUSE (1910-1988)

Dogs teach us
how to love
with an open
heart, and how
to live in joy.

AUTHOR UNKNOWN

Dogs... once they love, they love steadily, unchangingly, till their last breath.

ELIZABETH VON ARNIM
(1866-1941),
FROM "ALL THE DOGS
OF MY LIFE"

APRIL 8

There is something in him that evokes the greatest tenderness from people. His mere presence seems to bring out the better aspects of human nature.

ANTHONY DANIELS

SEPTEMBER 26

No home is complete
without a dog...
or rather, no home
is complete without
a dog, a chewed carpet,
a soiled bed, scratched
furniture....

STUART & LINDA MACFARLANE

It's as if they wake up every morning, and suddenly it's a new day: they are so alert and full of excitement and expectation, wondering what adventures lie in store for them. The world would certainly be a happier place if more humans were awake with such joy.

JACKIE STEWART, B. 1939

*If friends fail us, if the phone
is silent and the postman passes
Our dog will touch our knee,
and smile, and say, All the more
time for us to be together.
Come for a walk.
This is a splendid day.*

PAM BROWN, B.1928

Whoever else
thinks you are of little
worth – to your dog
you are the heart
of his universe.

PAM BROWN, B. 1928

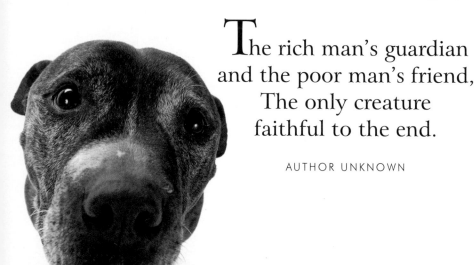

SEPTEMBER 24

The rich man's guardian
and the poor man's friend,
The only creature
faithful to the end.

AUTHOR UNKNOWN

"Whatever is, is good"
– your gracious creed.
You wear your joy
of living like a crown.

DOROTHY PARKER (1893-1967)

SEPTEMBER 23

Dogs have their own unique, loving ways to let us know that in times of crisis, in times of celebration, in times of daily life, we are not alone. A wag of the tail, a lick, and a hug, are some of the not too subtle ways that dogs express their love. Each day, a dog tells you, "I adore you!"

WILLARD SCOTT

APRIL 12

The average dog
has one request
to all humankind.
Love me.

HELEN EXLEY

There was a clear division of duties in the house; Lucky would sit, looking out of the window, guarding the house – I would do everything else.

STUART & LINDA MACFARLANE

A man's best friend
is his dog.

LORD BYRON (1788-1824)

A dog friend
just doesn't care
who you are –
fat or old or none
too steady on your pins.
Just so long as
you love him.

CHARLOTTE GRAY

To your dog, you are
more than just a friend;
you are the leader
of the pack, his protector,
his provider,
and an all-knowing god.

STUART & LINDA MACFARLANE

There's something so floppy
and droopy and heavy
and drowsy – so wriggly
and snuggly and nibbly about
a pup that you
wondered how
you ever managed
without him.

PAM BROWN, B.1928

APRIL 15

A puppy yearns
with every single
part of its being
to serve
and love you.
Love it in return.
Never betray its trust,
never despise its loyalty.

PAM BROWN, B.1928

The dog...never seems to change, not even when the end is there. Your coming through that front door remains, right to final tail wag, the single most significant event in the history of that moment – for the moment is all that they live for. And living for the moment is the secret that they give to us.

ROY MACGREGOR

Dogs bring out the
best in humankind.

PAMELA DUGDALE

SEPTEMBER 18

Our dogs trust us.
They don't question
our intentions.
They make us feel good
about ourselves,
and we are better
people because
of them.

MARI GAYATRI STEIN

APRIL 17

Sign on bulletin board:
"Puppies for sale:
The only love that
money can buy."

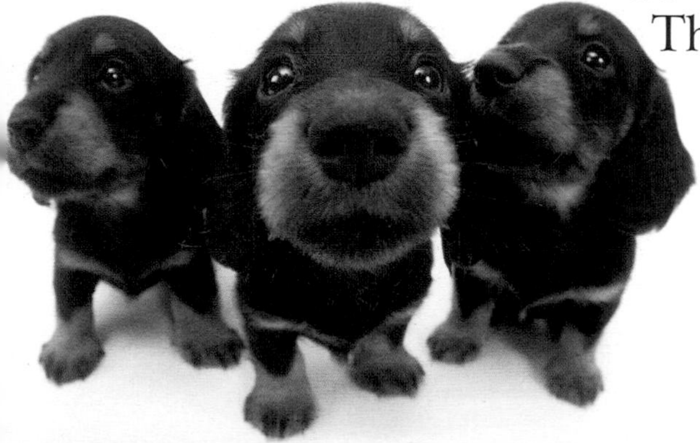

The agility of his ears
deserves a chapter to itself,
their eloquence reflecting
alertness, intent listening,
relaxation, or eating-mode,
when the ears become
horizontal like wing-mirrors.

VALERIE GROVE

Rarely did he take his beautiful, kind eyes off me... and wherever I went there he would be too, and wherever I sat he would... sit beside me – close, protecting me, his head on my knee.

ELIZABETH VON ARNIM (1866-1941), FROM "ALL THE DOGS OF MY LIFE"

SEPTEMBER 16

In its dreams
the most
domestic dog
is wild and free.

PAM BROWN, B.1928

Dogs, no matter
their breed, all have
an inner beauty.
They have kind,
gentle hearts
and a real need
for company
and affection.

STUART & LINDA MACFARLANE

SEPTEMBER 15

Dogs are great listeners. You can rattle on for hours about all your problems – they won't interrupt even once and will never, ever criticise.

STUART & LINDA MACFARLANE

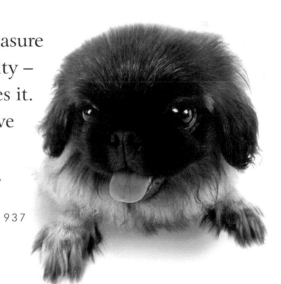

People need a measure
of happy simplicity –
and a dog supplies it.
Unqualified love
– and very
few demands.

CHARLOTTE GRAY, B.1937

If you have dogs,
then you're never on
your own.

ANTHEA TURNER, B. 1960

A life, a warmth,
an intelligence.
A kind companion.
A dog.

PAM BROWN, B.1928

SEPTEMBER 13

*Basil Harris qualifies
for the Guinness Book
of Wreckers, he has already eaten
two Chesterfields
(one leather and one dralon)
and three pairs of Charles
Jourdan shoes.*

JILLY COOPER, B.1937

Soft big eyes,
gentle and quiet.
She is patient and loving
– just what any
stressed-out
human needs.

HELEN EXLEY

A dog desires
affection more than
its dinner.
Well – almost.

PAM BROWN, B.1928

A dog believes you are
what you think you are.

JANE SWAN, B.1943

You never forget
a beloved dog.

MARK R. LEVIN

Every dog deserves
a smile, a word of admiration,
a little reassurance
– especially if he is very ugly
or very sad.

PAM BROWN, B.1928

All right, so I don't
know how to bury
my garden messes.
And I bark at everything.
But I love you, love you,
love you, and I will go
on loving you till
the day I die....

PAM BROWN, B.1928

Dogs come in
all shapes and sizes,
Yet every one,
you must agree,
Make humans
perfect company.

STUART & LINDA MACFARLANE

The dog goes to sleep in his basket. You wake up with him in the bed.

PETER GRAY, B.1928

A dog knows that if he sits in front of you long enough and pleads with every look and wag – you'll eventually give in and take him for a walk.

PAM BROWN, B.1928

SEPTEMBER 8

CHOOSING A PUPPY

He looked clumsy,
ugly, toothless,
but utterly adorable,
totally irresistible.
He just had to be mine.

MARGOT THOMSON

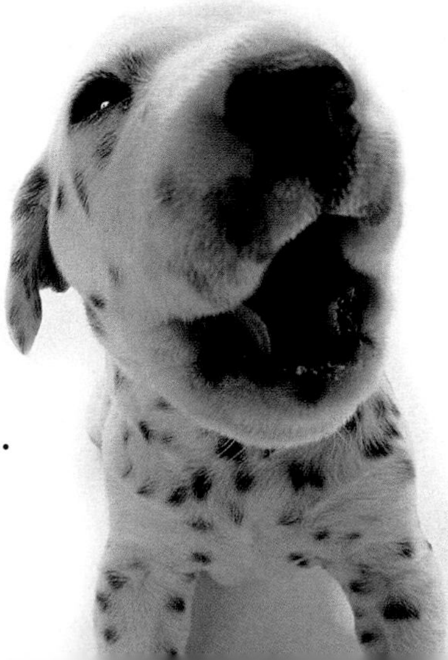

Puppies look like very small children whose mothers have bought a size or two too big clothes. To give them growing room.

MAYA V. PATEL, B.1943

"Beg!" I say.
"Sit!" I say.
"Down!" I say.
And he smiles –
and wanders off.

PAM BROWN, B.1928

...adorable little puppy
who will snuggle up
to you, nibble your ear,
gambol and romp
all over the place...
worming its way
into your heart,
making a slave of you....

BUSTER LLOYD-JONES

No matter
how little money
and how few
possessions you
own, having a dog
makes you rich.

LOUIS SABIN

What can we call them?!;
A huddle of pups? A wriggle of pups?
A squirm, a shove, a muddle of pups?
A drowse of pups? A sprawl of pups?
A totally out of this world of pups?
And all gathering the energy
to become a rush, a plunge,
a stampede of pups.

CLARA ORTEGA, B. 1955

I have found that when you are deeply troubled there are things you get from the silent devoted companionship of a dog that you can get from no other source.

DORIS DAY, B.1924

APRIL 30

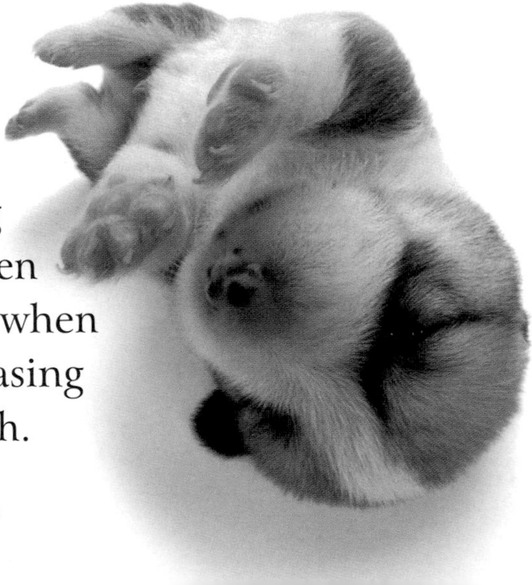

Your little dog
has never even seen
a rabbit – but watch when
he's asleep. He's chasing
down a mammoth.

PAM BROWN, B.1928

THERE IS NOTHING
SO GUILTY AS
A GUILTY DOG.

PAM BROWN, B.1928

The smart dog
quickly discovers that,
to get what he wants,
one mournful look
is much more effective
than a frenzy of barking.

STUART & LINDA MACFARLANE

The one absolutely unselfish friend that man can have in this selfish world, the one that never deserts him, the one that never proves ungrateful or treacherous, is his dog.

SENATOR GEORGE
G. VEST (1830-1904)

A dog likes to sit
under the dining table.
Just in case.

PAM BROWN, B.1928

SEPTEMBER 2

When the world
is at its dismal,
dullest, darkest your dog
will insist on his walk
– and cheer you back
to sanity.

PETER GRAY, B.1928

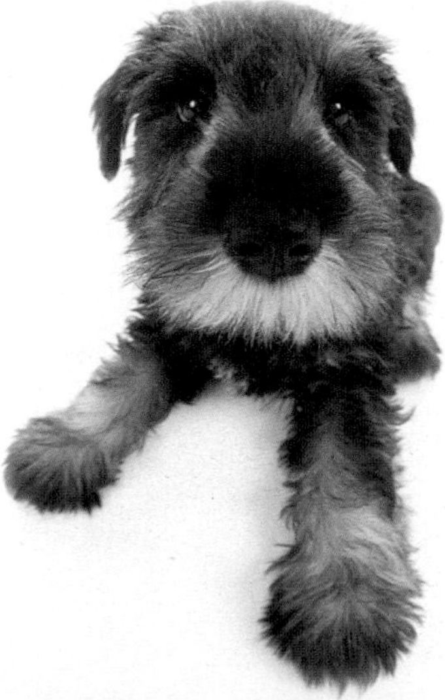

W believe
in ourselves
because of the trust
our puppy has in us.

MARGOT THOMSON

His head on my knee
can heal
my human hurts.

GENE HILL

Some dogs, having
endured appalling suffering,
are so broken, kindness
can never cure them.
And some
come out of horror
capable of trust
and find at last the world
a happy place.

PAMELA DUGDALE

AUGUST 31

[Your dog] never knows that you have been mean or jealous or grasping. It encourages you to be kindly and when you respond, it loves you.

SIR JAMES WALPOLE

Old age means realising
you will never own all
the dogs you wanted to.

JOE GORES

Little puppies
in pet shops should
have a warning
sign above their cages,
"Do not look
into my eyes
for I will kidnap
your heart."

STUART & LINDA MACFARLANE

How strange to think Dog was once simply
Dog. For see how we have squashed him
and stretched him. Yet inside every variation is
that first and utterly basic Dog.

PAMELA DUGDALE

AUGUST 29

It is always
disconcerting
to carry on
a conversation
with a dog
whose eyes are
totally invisible.

PAM BROWN, B.1928

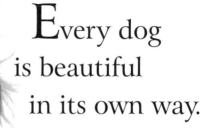

Every dog
is beautiful
in its own way.

STUART & LINDA MACFARLANE

AUGUST 28

Heaven goes by favor.
If it went by merit,
you would stay out
and your dog would go in!

MARK TWAIN (1835-1910)

MAY 8

A DOG WILL CONTINUE TO TRUST WHEN IT HAS BEEN BETRAYED.

CHARLOTTE GRAY, B.1937

Oh, the saddest
of sights in
a world of sin
is a little lost
pup with his tail
tucked in!

ARTHUR GUITERMAN

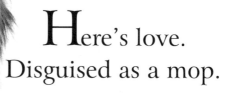

MAY **9**

H'ere's love.
Disguised as a mop.

PETER GRAY, B.1928

AUGUST 26

When you come home your dog says "You're home! I love you. I love you. I love you."

PAM BROWN, B.1928

If a dog's prayers were answered, bones would fall from the sky.

PROVERB

Even asleep,
he will detect someone
scraping out the last remnants
of Marmite from the jar
in the kitchen four floors
below and thunder downstairs
to lick it clean.

TREVOR GROVE

...if he wanted a dog biscuit, he simply sat
near the box of biscuits and silently
stared at one or the other of us.
If he not merely wanted a biscuit
but felt it was positively his right
to have one, the silent stare
was accompanied by a lowering
of the head...

GEORGE PITCHER, FROM
"THE DOGS WHO CAME TO STAY"

BRAVE LITTLE FELLOW
He was only a little puppy
when he took on the whole world
to defend me.
He was absurdly brave.
And it was there and then
that I determined to return
his love and be all that
he expected of me.

HELEN THOMSON

The world
would be a sadder
place without puppies.

PAM BROWN, B.1928

She has crawled into
the deepest corners
of my heart, the places that
hold the most love –
and the most pain.

CAROLINE KNAPP

Just a scruffy little dog...
And yet you are the best,
the kindest friend
anyone could have.

MARGOT THOMSON

AUGUST22

Show a dog
AN OUNCE OF LOVE
AND HE'LL BE
YOUR FRIEND FOR LIFE.

STUART & LINDA MACFARLANE

Happy is the dog who has found a kind human – he will forever have someone to tickle his tummy.

STUART & LINDA
MACFARLANE

They invite us
to be exuberant
and playful
without needing
a reason.

MARI GAYATRI STEIN

MAY 15

'Tis sweet to hear the
watch-dog's honest bark
Bay deep-mouth'd welcome
as we draw near home;
'Tis sweet to know there is
an eye will mark
Our coming, and look
brighter when we come.

LORD BYRON (1788-1824)

There is invariably
one dimwit
in the litter –
but what he lacks
in sagacity he usually
makes up for in
bumbling charm.

CHARLOTTE GRAY

Poor dog! He was faithful and kind
to be sure, And he constantly
loved me although I was poor;
When the sour-looking folk
sent me heartless away, I had
always a friend in my poor dog Tray.

THOMAS CAMPBELL (1763-1854)

AUGUST 19

My friend has a fine watch dog. At any suspicious noise he wakes the dog and the dog begins to bark.

LEOPOLD FECHTNER

...we simply loved them with all our hearts; we perhaps even loved them – I'm not ashamed to say – beyond all reason. And they loved us, too, completely, no holds barred. Such love is perhaps the best thing life has to offer.

GEORGE PITCHER, FROM
"THE DOGS WHO CAME TO STAY"

A well-trained dog
will make no attempt
to share your lunch.
He will just make you
feel so guilty that
you cannot enjoy it.

HELEN THOMSON

Dogs bring
special gifts to
the lives of those
who live with them.

ALLEN & LINDA ANDERSON

Many a day
he pulled me away
from my solitude, anger,
laziness and greed...
He covered me
with wet sappy kisses
and warmed me
with big
howling welcomes.

ROMA IHNATOWYCZ

A dog is love for a lifetime.

PAM BROWN, B.1928

AUGUST 16

I f the doctor insists that you try exercise, acquire a puppy. He will take over the entire treatment.

JENNY DE VRIES

It is hard to imagine
that these flubsy little scraps
– all feet and tail and belly –
will grow into disciplined
and beautiful dogs.
But they will.

PETER GRAY, B.1928

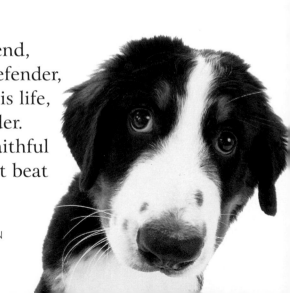

AUGUST 15

He is your friend,
your partner, your defender,
your dog. You are his life,
his love, his leader.
He will be yours, faithful
and true, to the last beat
of his heart.

AUTHOR UNKNOWN

MAY 21

No one appreciates
the very special genius
of your conversation
as a dog does.

CHRISTOPHER MORLEY
(1890-1957)

"*Get away, Ugly,
you beastly dog!*"
*he would say.
And the dog would
be apparently in
an ecstasy of enjoyment
at being called
anything at all.*

SIR JAMES WALPOLE

I realized, it was not I who was looking
at the dogs, but the dogs who
looked at me, and each dog
with the same look in the eyes...
the same hope,
the same hopelessness.
"Can I come with you?
Can I be your dog?
Can't I be your dog?
No?"

ERIC PARKER
FROM "BEST OF DOGS"

AUGUST 13

If you are patient
with your human
he will soon learn
a few dog words
such as dinner,
fetch and walkies.

STUART & LINDA MACFARLANE

A dog is a smile
and a wagging tail.
What is in between
doesn't
matter much.

CLARA ORTEGA, B.1955

How sensible.
He looks you in
the eye and sees you
as an equal.
He is courteous and kind.
A gentleman.

PAM BROWN, B.1928

What a very small,
what a very ordinary dog.
No pedigree
and very little looks –
But a creature full
of life and love.

PAMELA DUGDALE

AUGUST 11

Sometimes
doing absolutely
nothing is
quite enough
for one day.

STUART & LINDA MACFARLANE

MAY 25

"Some enchanted evening..."
And so it is with pups
and people.
A seething
mass of small,
yapping,
prancing puppies
– and one stands out
like a star.
Your puppy.

PAM BROWN, B.1928

There always
seems to be more skin
to a puppy
than it can
possibly need.

MAYA V. PATEL, B.1943

Puppies are nature's remedy for feeling unloved...
plus numerous other ailments of life.

RICHARD ALLAN PALM,
FROM "MARTHA, PRINCESS OF DIAMONDS"

All they ask for
is the most basic shelter,
food and water, and in return
they give us unbounded,
unflinching affection.

LEO MCKINSTRY, FROM
"DAILY MAIL", FEBRUARY 18, 2003

What are little puppies made of?
30% cuteness
29% mischief
28% affection
10% soft fur
3% innocence

STUART & LINDA MACFARLANE

Charley likes to get up early,
and he likes me
to get up early too.
And why shouldn't he?
Right after his breakfast
he goes back to sleep.

JOHN STEINBECK
(1902-1968)

Pug is come!

– come to fill up the void
left by false
and narrow-hearted friends.
I see already that he is without envy,
hatred, or malice –
that he will betray no secrets,
and feel neither pain at my success
nor pleasure in my chagrin.

GEORGE ELIOT
[MARY ANN EVANS] (1819-1880)

I am going to
be a guard dog.
Eventually.
I think.
But not yet.

PAM BROWN, B.1928

MAY 29

A puppy can smell
dinner through double
glazing and heavy oaken
doors and brick
and concrete
and a casserole dish.

PAMELA DUGDALE

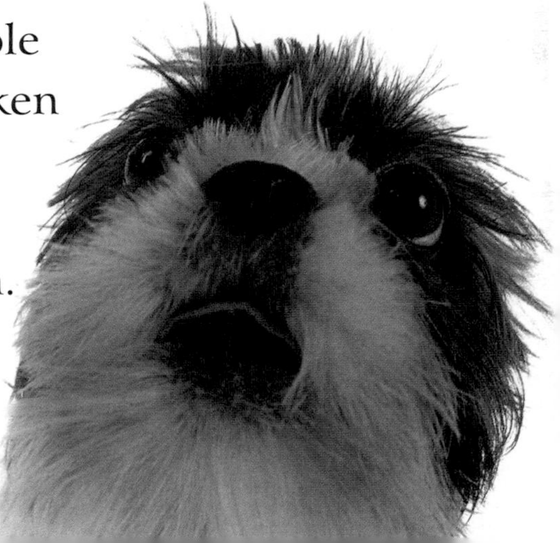

AUGUST 6

There is no psychiatrist in the world like a puppy...

BERN WILLIAMS

Dog's maxim
ON RELAXATION:
The secret to being completely relaxed
is to have a human
to do all the worrying for you.

STUART & LINDA MACFARLANE

His enthusiasm
for each new day
was infectious.

KAREN WHEELER

There is so much we can learn from Tuts.
About loyalty and love.
And a complete absence of selfishness.
Tuts seems to exist to give us
happiness. I know that when
I'm stressed out, all I need
to do is summon him for
a back-scratch.

SHOBHA DÉ, FROM "SPEEDPOST"

Who needs words
when your eyes and tail
can speak for you?

PAM BROWN, B.1928

JUNE 1

A dog trusts deeply
and so is easily betrayed.

CHARLOTTE GRAY, B.1937

Java taught me
how to be
a better person
by being an example
of unconditional love
and peace.

SAGE LEWIS

"Won't be long" means nothing to a dog. All he knows is that you are GONE.

JANE SWAN, B.1943

AUGUST 2

A cat does not betray the fact that he has done something diabolical. A dog is racked with guilt – and so gives the game away.

PETER GRAY

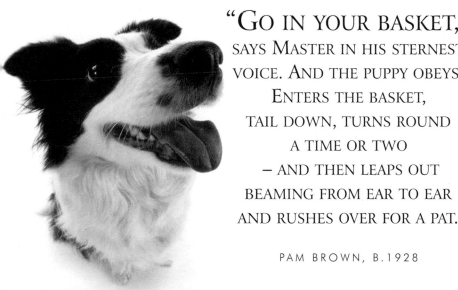

JUNE 3

"GO IN YOUR BASKET,"
SAYS MASTER IN HIS STERNEST
VOICE. AND THE PUPPY OBEYS.
ENTERS THE BASKET,
TAIL DOWN, TURNS ROUND
A TIME OR TWO
– AND THEN LEAPS OUT
BEAMING FROM EAR TO EAR
AND RUSHES OVER FOR A PAT.

PAM BROWN, B.1928

I, who had had my heart full
for hours, took advantage
of an early moment
of solitude, to cry very bitterly.
Suddenly a little hairy head thrust
itself from behind my
pillow into my face...
drying the tears as they came.

ELIZABETH BARRETT BROWNING
(1806-1861)

...Foss took this ancient
responsibility very seriously.
He used to chase aeroplanes,
rushing out into the garden
and barking at them till they
flew away.
Then he would come in again,
breathing rather heavily,
with an expression of satisfaction
at a job well done.

CELIA HADDON,
FROM "FAITHFUL TO THE END"

Your little dog
gulps down his food.
Before the hyenas
and the vultures arrive.

PAM BROWN, B.1928

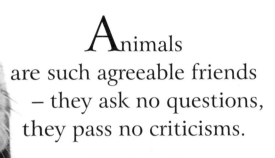

Animals
are such agreeable friends
– they ask no questions,
they pass no criticisms.

GEORGE ELIOT
[MARY ANN EVANS] (1819-1880)

"He'll grow out of it" has more hope than certainty.

PAM BROWN, B.1928

I am unable to imagine how anybody who lives with an intelligent and devoted dog can ever be lonely.

ELIZABETH VON ARNIM (1866-1941),
FROM "ALL THE DOGS OF MY LIFE"

A dog wakens your heart to joy and companionship – and to sorrow.

PAM BROWN, B.1928

How can any of us
explain how we feel...
in the early morning,
when the animal we have
chosen to share our lives is
standing... waiting,
to renew the pleasure
of our presence.

JOYCE STRANGER

"Oh! Please! Tell me how
I get out of these amazing clothes.
I've been struggling with them
for hours and hours.
I don't think they're me at all...
or are they?
I am sort of gorgeous,
and look kinda cute, don't I?"

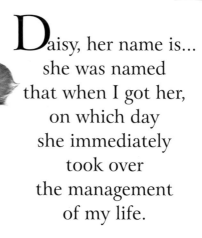

JULY 28

Daisy, her name is...
she was named
that when I got her,
on which day
she immediately
took over
the management
of my life.

DOROTHY PARKER (1893-1967)

Fence in your garden,
block all gaps with wood
and wire. Spread
the lawn with toys. And after
a while the man next door
will knock on your door
– a jubilant puppy
squirming in his arms.

PAM BROWN, B.1928

A pup is like a baby. It goes on trusting long after it has been betrayed.

PAM BROWN, B.1928

He is convinced
that life is good
– and always will be.
Never disillusion him!

PAMELA DUGDALE

And when we bury our face
in our hands and wish
we had never been born ...
he looks up at you
with his big, true eyes,
and says with them,
"Well, you've always got me."

JEROME K. JEROME (1859-1927)

...I felt a silent current of love
from him – strong, steady
and deep – unceasingly
flowing to me...
For someone who has never
had this kind of experience
with a pet, there are no words
to adequately explain it.

SUSAN RACE

JULY 25

A dog can talk you into most things – silently.

PAM BROWN, B.1928

The reward of owning
a well-behaved, loving
and intelligent dog
is beyond measure.
Those who have owned
such a dog
are truly blessed.

BARBARA WOODHOUSE (1910-1988),
FROM "THE FAMILY PET"

Whether I have been away for a working week or just two minutes across the road buying a bottle of milk from the village store, Buster always welcomes me home as if I am a hero returning from the wars.

ROY HATTERSLEY

This is the pup
that will worry a glove to death.
Kill a shoe.
Rip a toilet roll to shreds
– and run a mile
if it sees a mouse.

PAM BROWN, B.1928

Wе must choose
the strongest pup, the
cleverest, the most active.
So why do we choose,
the most helpless, tiny,
tiny dog, all eyes
and rumpled fur?

PAM BROWN, B.1928

JUNE 13

NOT CARNEGIE, VANDERBILT
AND ASTOR TOGETHER
COULD HAVE RAISED
MONEY ENOUGH TO BUY
A QUARTER SHARE
IN MY LITTLE DOG.

ERNEST THOMPSON SETON (1860-1946)

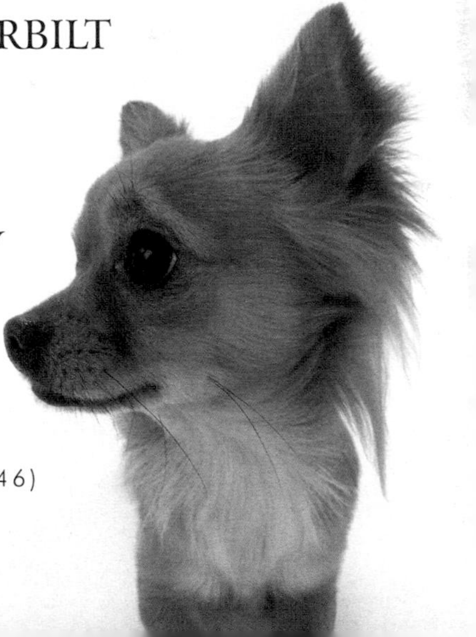

JULY 22

He is loyalty itself.
He has taught
me the meaning
of devotion.
With him,
I know a secret comfort
and a private peace.

GENE HILL

JUNE 14

MONUMENT TO LORD BYRON'S
DOG BOATSWAIN

BEAUTY WITHOUT VANITY,
STRENGTH WITHOUT
INSOLENCE, COURAGE
WITHOUT FEROCITY,
AND ALL THE VIRTUES
OF MAN WITHOUT HIS VICES.

Your dog stands
and quietly whines;
it's time to drop
your worries
and take the little guy
for a walk.

HELEN EXLEY

A dull day, a sad day,
a frustrating day –
    but everything seems
bright when a small
    furry object hurls
into your arms
    and tells you how very glad
    he is to see you home.

PAM BROWN, B.1928

Even a puppy
will endure
the unendurable
out of love.

PAM BROWN, B.1928

A dog will never
break your heart,
betray your trust,
or abandon you
when you are needy and
afraid, in the throes
of madness, or drowning
in the lagoon
of your emotions.

MARI GAYATRI STEIN, FROM
"UNLEASHING YOUR INNER DOG"

Thousands of generations of dogs have, in their heart of hearts, believed that one day, if they listen hard enough, and concentrate, they will eventually master human speech.

MAYA V. PATEL, B.1943

Dogs are always more delighted than anyone else in the family to see you return from work.

SALLY MORRIS

THE LOVE FOR
A WELL-CHOSEN
DOG CAN TRANSCEND
LIFE ITSELF.

STANLEY COREN

Dog, n. *A kind of additional or subsidiary Deity designed to catch the overflow and surplus of the world's worship.*

AMBROSE BIERCE
(1842-1914)

Montmorency's ambition in life is to get in the way and be sworn at. If he can squirm in anywhere where he particularly is not wanted... he feels his day has not been wasted.

JEROME K. JEROME

To hold a living creature, to learn its loveliness, to feel its heart beat in our hands, to know its trust, is at last to understand that we are kin. Is to rejoice in life. Is to lose all loneliness.

PAM BROWN, B.1928

A dog cannot read print,
but he can read
your eyes, your mouth,
your fingertips,
very well indeed.

PAM BROWN, B.1928

Dogs have stolen our hearts, our homes and our wallets, not necessarily in that order...

AUTHOR UNKNOWN

*Tugs brought new meaning
to the term "adoration".
Wherever I went, he wanted
to be there too.
He never took his eyes off me
and with a simple glance
in his direction, his whole body
wagged with happiness.*

SUSAN RACE

A dog smiles
with its whole face –
ears, eyes, nose,
whiskers,
mouth, tongue.

PAM BROWN, B.1928

DOG'S MAXIM
ON FRIENDSHIP:
Your very best friend
is whoever is holding
the bone.

STUART & LINDA MACFARLANE

He's a brilliant, ordinary, incredible companion and my little prince.

ROXANNE WILLEM SNOPEK

JULY 13

Dogs have a way
of bringing you back
to earth. Their affection
shames pretense.
They are guileless.

GARRISON KEILLOR, B.1942

*W*hat jolly chaps they are!
They are much superior to human beings
as companions. They do
not quarrel or argue with you.
They never talk about themselves,
but listen to
you while you talk
about yourself...

JEROME K. JEROME
(1859-1927)

One cute little puppy can turn a king
into a jester.

STUART & LINDA
MACFARLANE

A dog can be more
than a companion
in pain and loss
and loneliness.
It can be a dear
and trusted comforter.

PAMELA DUGDALE

I wag my tail and your blues fade away, I snuggle close and frown turns to smile, I play catch and your world fills with laughter. And all I ask in return, is two meals a day… and all your love.

STUART & LINDA MACFARLANE

JUNE 25

Give a pup
a home and
a little love
and he will give
you his heart
forever.

PAM BROWN, B.1928

If your dog decides
it is time for his walk
– there's not
a great deal you
can do about it.

PAMELA DUGDALE

JUNE 26

One has to be very
devoted to dogs
to endure the loving
attention of
a slobberer.

CHARLOTTE GRAY

A dog appreciates
the person
who knows all
the right places
to scratch.

CHARLOTTE GRAY

*A happy dog,
however young,
however small holds
its head high –
being loved, being wanted,
being your companion.*

PAM BROWN, B.1928

*Humankind is
drawn to dogs
because they are so like
ourselves – bumbling,
affectionate, confused,
easily disappointed,
grateful for kindness...*

PAM BROWN, B.1928

JUNE 28

N ever bite when
a simple growl will do.
Never growl when
looking cute will do.
No matter what you've
done wrong, always try
to make it look like
the cat did it.

STUART & LINDA MACFARLANE

However large
the house a puppy
will always
be underfoot.

PAMELA DUGDALE

I believe by far the greatest number are owned just for the sheer delight of having a lovely creature round the house to be admired, to admire you...

BARBARA WOODHOUSE
(1910-1988)

Your dog just
doesn't notice
that you are old or ill
or unsuccessful.
To him
you are perfect.

PAM BROWN, B.1928

Keesha was my friend, my confidant, my angel and, ultimately, my teacher.

SUSAN CHERNAK MCELROY,
FROM "ANIMALS AS TEACHERS
AND HEALERS"

When all other friends
desert, he remains.
When riches take wings,
and reputation falls
to pieces, he is as
constant in his love
as the sun in its journey
through the heavens.

SENATOR
GEORGE G. VEST
(1830-1904)

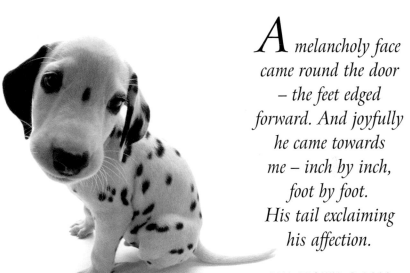

JULY 1

A melancholy face came round the door – the feet edged forward. And joyfully he came towards me – inch by inch, foot by foot. His tail exclaiming his affection.

PAM BROWN, B.1928

JULY 4

RULES FOR MY HUMAN
*Do not dig up my bones
while gardening.
Keep to your own part of the bed.
Be attentive to my every need.
Take me for walks
every time I ask!*

STUART & LINDA MACFARLANE

Most dogs don't think
they are human;
they know they are.

JANE SWAN, B.1943

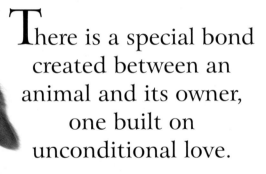

There is a special bond created between an animal and its owner, one built on unconditional love.

LEO MCKINSTRY,
FROM "DAILY MAIL",
FEBRUARY 18, 2003